Simultaneous Everything

Simultaneous Everything

Kevin Acers

Lampadina Press

Also by Kevin Acers:

Time Machine: Prose Poems & Vignettes
Dead Mouse Poems
*The Murder of Crows and Other Quirky Poems**
*Zippy Zappy: Diminutive Poetry**
I am Not a Dog and Other Poems

*Oklahoma Book Award finalist

Lampadina Press

ISBN: 978-1-7357551-0-6

Printed in the United States of America

For Peter

(1959 - 2020)

Contents

Aphorisms

Rhetorical Questions

Simultaneous Everything

The distinction between past, present, and future is only an illusion – even if a stubborn one.

Albert Einstein

Everything is everywhere.

Lourens Baas Becking

The Immediate Now

The distant past and the distant future
are no more distant than the distant present,

and some might say they are no less immediate
than the immediate now.

The Truth Is

I am not a hunter of ducks.
I am not a roller derby girl
with a fierce grimace
and an elbow held up high
poised to assault a competitor.
I am not a connoisseur of shellfish.
I am not a monkey
strapped into a capsule marked
with the letters CCCP atop a rocket
about to be launched into orbit
where I am doomed to die.
I am not a young boy hoeing around
melon vines to aerate the soil
and decapitate weeds.
I am not a beautiful meteorologist
named Cindy.
I am not an athlete spitting
brown tobacco-stained saliva
onto the grass.
I am not a carny whose beefy hands
are blackened with grease
from repairing the machinery
of a crippled Ferris wheel.
I am not a large animal veterinarian.
I am not a disillusioned puppeteer.
I am not a funeral director
experiencing the effects
of generalized anxiety disorder.
I am not a Jesuit.
I am not a small town reporter
who drinks gin with lunch,

but most notably
I am not a Tony Award nominee.

Maybe next year.

Aspirations

I would like to toss handfuls of crepe myrtle petals from a hot air balloon
and watch till the last one floats to the ground.

I would like to plant wisteria on a fertile moon and watch
as its vines grow and slow-dance like tendrils in the sea.

I would like to be steam rising from a hot spring far from human eyes.

I would like to dive through the crust of the earth with open eyes
and startle the roots and the worms, swallowing dirt as I go.

I would like to listen to my own birth-cries while I scatter my ashes
with help from the wind.

I would like to shrink impossibly small
and frolick, miniaturized, among the molecules.

I would like to dwell on an edible mountain, munch on stones
as juicy as grapes, and gaze at the Milky Way.

I would like to achieve perfect perception of temporal, physical truth:
simultaneous everything.

Secret Society

Bright blue urine is weird
and unexpectedly pretty.
While some might suspect
extraterrestrial origins,
others among us know
what exactly for Earthlings it means.
(We need a secret handshake.)

My Wife Walks in the Garden

She tilts her face upward, eyes gently closed
as she enjoys the sensations of Spring, and smiles.
Three white geese are flying overhead.
These swan-like creatures feel shame
when they see her upturned face
and the ease of its beauty.
They fold their wings to cover their eyes
and drop from the sky, each with a similar thud.

Creation Story

i.

Steel, flesh, and wood
interact
as an old man
absent-mindedly
whittles a stick.

ii.

Bright raw shavings
curl courtesy of
the knife's kinesis
with each lazy whip
of the old man's hand.

iii.

The shavings briefly float
before they fall,
and in that interval
a new world fills
the moment.

iv.

Who is to say
that moments like this
are not everlasting?

Rehearsing the Apocalypse

Water in the clouds
separates itself
before falling.

It slams into
the pavement
like a city of suicides.

Katydids Tonight

Let me hear the song of the katydids tonight
and rest while the thick summer air
climbs in through open windows.

Let the sticky sweat dampen my elbow creases
without, somehow, making me scream.
Calm me, katydids.

Serenade gently this time of the year
when acceptance is crucial for sleep.
The comfort you sing of is a myth I believe in.

Where in August 1989 is the Epicenter of Joy?

Wild onions or fireflies in the hills,
street tacos or a dancing monkey,
a kite or a clock,
fruit bats or a flying buttress,
a rose petal's texture or pebbles,
bronchitis or a canoe?

The answer is what happens during a lunar eclipse viewed behind a farmhouse with friends drinking sangria when two wander away down a quiet road in the nearby woods.

Beelzebub Eats

Beelzebub eats
cauliflower
for breakfast,

soaks it in a marinade
then reheats it
for lunch

and tells
his friends
it is rich

in protein,
high in fiber,
and made

from the souls
of renegade
Lutherans.

One Wears a Hat

Imagine if you can a hat
with a hidden mechanism
of magnets and springs.

Upon placing the hat on one's head
the moving parts *sproing!*
from inside the hatband,
piercing one's skin and
surprising the meat underneath.
Affixing itself with small sharp hooks
to the stone-like bone, the hat
becomes a permanent feature.

No photographs will reveal one's face
unshaded by the brim of the hat.
Shampooing becomes
impossible and combs absurd.

The hat is a part of the head
as the head is a part of the neck
as the neck is a part of the back
and the back the belly, and all the rest.

Romance becomes as futile
as a strange dream one forgets
upon waking.

"My marriage is to a hat," one writes
with a finger in the moisture
on a windowpane.

One then mumbles, "My hat is a trap."
Countless remembered comments
echo in one's mind.
"Nice hat!" "Love your hat!"
"Where'd you get that hat!"

As an afterthought, one writes again
with a finger on the glass:
"My _______ is a hat."
For several subsequent hours
one fills in the blank.

After a Time

All that is left is a dampness. Minerals will have separated themselves from the body's fluids and having more weight will have sunk into the soil. The water molecules will soon evaporate. They will rise to intermingle with similar vaporous cells and coalesce into clouds. These butterfly clouds will float aloft in obeyance with the winds until one day in pregnant fullness they all collapse, a wonderful catastrophe. The water falls as rain, soaks back into the soil, returning to moisten the minerals waiting with a patient thirst.

My Parents' Ghosts

The look of bemusement
on my poor mother's face
while I'd brush her teeth
stares from the mirror
as I brush my own years later.
As if it's a competition,
my father's laughter
bounces in my throat.

Visiting Jennie

While her friends were preparing food inside, I capsized a canoe I was sharing with Jennie in the pond behind the house. Laughing awkwardly, we hoisted ourselves back into the boat. Embarrassed and shivering, I would sit through dinner in wet pants – cold and uncomfortable, wishing to be invisible – complimenting the beauty of Maine.

Tonic for Troubling Dreams

Filter your oxygen supply
with a net woven of hairs
that resemble the hair
of your earliest memories
(likely that of your mother).
The source of these hairs
can be almost anything:
a spider, a rabbit, a cousin,
a corpse, a pasta machine.

Wear the net like a sock that
fully envelops your head.
Your hair-filtered oxygen
will aerate not just your lungs
and blood supply, but also
through mysterious means
the saliva you swallow
while you are sleeping,
to which it will give a flavor
beyond bitterness or ketchup's
sinister sweetness.

And then your dreams
will unfold without joy, terror,
love, angst, or inspiration,
all of which may be the same
in the blur of sleep.

You may wake up and regret
that you remember nothing.

Into the Hollow Gloom

Facing uncertainty
and seeing no hope
is not a cause for despair.

Walking into
an opaque fog
is all we ever do.

Cautiously or boldly,
we head into
the hollow gloom.

What we encounter
is not always
horrible.

Human Ink

While I am
not indelible,
I am all right
with that –
neither
is the rain.

Lazy Autumn

Leaves descend like strange snow
or like drunken paratroopers
booted half-conscious
from planes, dozing
while they fall.

Deciding to Float

If weary of circular movement
from rowing with an oar
on a single side of the boat,
let the paddle slip into the lake.

Allow your arms to dangle.
Drift at rest, and gently –
never mind direction or speed
or cardiovascular oomph.

Gaze across the water at the insects
skimming its surface, and at its distant banks,
and as the sky begins to deepen its blue,
at the emergent light of the moon.

Drink coffee from a thermos
until dawn. Then draw yourself
into the water, wish the empty boat well,
and find your way to the shore.

I See Small Fish

I see small fish
swimming in her eyes,
fancy-tailed guppies,
one in each eye,
hovering sideways
and waving their tails
like fabulous flags.
Strangely, I am not
even slightly surprised.

Drinking Song

Gulp by gulp
the Thai iced coffee
sings of itself,
full-throated
and boisterous.
I rattle the glass
like a shy child
shakes a tambourine.

The Messiah Visits Southern Oklahoma

Having some time on his hands, the Messiah wandered forty days and nights in the part of the world where he inexplicably found himself. This happened to be a stretch of southern Oklahoma. He picked up trash along a state highway for a while, not with any sense of mission, but because intuitively it just felt right. One sweltering day he stopped in at a Dairy Queen. At random, he ordered a dip cone. He watched as the bored teenaged girl behind the counter swirled vanilla ice cream from a machine into a cone, then tumped it upside down into a vat of liquid chocolate, turned it upright again, and handed it to the Messiah. He thought this was miraculous. He marveled at the chocolate's immediately forming a hard shell on the surface of the cold ice cream with a charming twist on top. He took it to a table, sat, and ate of it. It was good. Sitting there, his mind flashed on a strange vision in which he was overturning tables and vendors' stalls crowding the temple grounds in Jerusalem. "Could never do that here," he observed. "This table is bolted to the floor." He felt less cheered than irritated by the red-and-white color theme of the Dairy Queen's plastic décor so didn't linger. After finishing his dip cone he wiped his hands on his pants – he was wearing faded trousers made of denim – and headed back outside. The sun was starting to set. The asphalt on the parking lot was still resonating heat. Across the road he saw a sign indicating that a place called Durant was 24 miles to the east. With a shrug, he started walking.

Marooned Potatoes

Marooned potatoes
never shout for help.
They do not panic
or weep. They typically
do not fret about rotting.
They do not concern
themselves with possible
rescue, or gather materials
for building a raft.
They settle into a mode
of calm acceptance.

They rot anyway.

Cartography

At the sight of an ample bottom
my mind recalls the Mercator projection:
all those magnificent continents,
highest elevations of the ocean's floor,
rise from the sloshing sea.

Lacking Certain Talents

Lying in bed
I stare dumbfounded
at the empty space
forty inches above me.
I ponder the disheartening
truth that the joyful arts
in my dissipated dream
are imaginary ones.

Awake, I have lost
the ability to improvise
brilliant, explosive ballet;
to lean down and forward
into a piano's keys
to produce beautiful
spontaneous concertos;
to engage small birds
in meaningful chatter
as they frolick in the bath.

Feeling drugged, I stir,
moving my heavy legs
like an awkward child
on a bicycle, kicking
off my bedsheets.
I clumsily rise,
abandoning grace,
and walk into the day
regretting my lack
of those talents.

The Walk-in Office

I met a guy who looks like you,
he said, the last time I was here.
Yes, I said, I know the guy you mean.
He sat right there, where you are now, he said.
Right, I said. That is how it works here.
We take turns sitting here and meeting you,
and, of course, the others who come here.
Yes, he said, trying to absorb it. Yes,
I see. Everyone takes a turn,
and everyone looks a lot like you.
So how can I help you, I said, and he
pulled out a gun and shot me in the stomach.
This is precisely the reason, I gasped,
that we take turns.

The Infinite Now

The notion of eternity confounds me.
Forever is such a long time,
as abstract as math's highest number.
But what if forever unfolds all at once?
One impossibly complex moment,
non-linear, and we are in its midst,
what happened billions of days ago and
what will happen in a billion more.
It's all happening now – but now is big.
One temporal explosion, one deep moment,
one place, one time, all of everything occurring,
imagined, remembered, perceived, forgotten,
unnoticed by all who have or will have
or have experienced a manifestation of change:
everything ever to happen happening Now
in all spaces of physical reality, mental perception,
and inanimate unconsciousness,
all one simultaneous everything.

Eating a Dwarf Planet

Drizzling honey onto an English muffin on this morning of the equinox, I watch as it wriggles its way from a circular swirl, creeping into the open mouths of the bread's miniature craters. The thick amber liquid seeps just beneath the surface as if into the crust of a planet. This must be what it would be like, I ponder as I lift it for a bite, to be a space monster devouring Pluto after slicing it into sections and coating it with alien goo. Behind me the length of my glowing body extends far into the vacuum of space as, here up front, I chew with eager indulgence.

Even If No One Hears

Miles from would-be witnesses
of the sentient sort with eyeballs
and eardrums and things

thunder grumbles at mighty heights.
The atmosphere cracks like glass,
and a mass of clouds vomits

hurling a great lake's worth
of violent rain
storming into the sea.

No one is there to hear.
Nobody sees. Nobody knows.
But still.

My Abecedarian

My abecedarian
consists of
twenty-six pebbles
slowly dropped
one by one
into a pond
in order to behold
the water's
expanding pattern
of circles.

I, Asteroid

i.
An asteroid sails
for two billion years
through the Moment.

ii.
An asteroid, I do not
differentiate myself
from biological things.

iii.
The stars' applause
and white-hot lights
do not distract this asteroid.

iv.
My path in focus,
I angle past planets
without a single hello.

v.
An asteroid surrenders
to Physics and its
splendid choreography.

vi.
I, asteroid, tumble through
space unhindered
by the friction of regrets.

vii.
The Moment
and I are enjoying
our conjugal visit.

Alchemy

A boy. A dog, a bicycle.

A shining Self emerges
from combining
basic elements with
just the right timing.

Anonymous Thomas

Thomas Thomas is the oddly redundant name
of a man whose boyhood friends would call him Tommy.
Taunting harassers, in turn, would call him Tom-tom.
His mother called him nothing but Thomas except
when perturbed, and then it was "*Thomas* Thomas!"

His wrung-out mother, when she'd seen him
at childbirth all beet-red and bleating
thought it a dignified name. His father
was agreeably indifferent. He had mused that
at least it would be easy for the boy
when he learned to write his name.

Thomas was not ashamed of his name as a child,
but he was ashamed in general. Some boys just are.
The inevitable bullies who whiffed his scent
conjured a rallying cry – *Beat the Tom-tom!* –
and they did whenever they could.

A quiet bookkeeper now called Tom, he sometimes
contemplates death, casually and observant
like one thinks of an apple while chewing a mouthful.

When the time comes, he has decided, his headstone
will simply read THOS. So appropriately simple.

Moored and Afloat

I seem to be
in the middle of me,
not exactly captive,
not precisely free.

Feels a bit weird
to be both apart from
and fully entrenched
in me.

Perhaps this
is how we are
all inclined
to be.

Fuzzy's Tacos

Taco shells crunch as
beans and diced tomatoes
tumble through my fingers.

I relish the savory cheese,
the habanero salsa sting,
the citrus tang of lime.

A young woman sits nearby,
her light brown skin the backdrop
for tattoos of elephants.

Her elephants' impatience
unnerves me. Ready to stomp,
they glare at me, eager for a meal.

Who is Your Uyinene Mrwetyana?

Who is your Uyinene
Mrwetyana, the one
whose vicious rape
rouses in you
an outrage
whose unshakable
intensity steals
your breath and rattles
your windows hard,
hard and incessantly?
The flash of a face –
I will not share
her name.

The Languages of Trees

Poets demonstrate this shortcoming:
writing in human language is an underachievement.
I would love to write in the dialect of a sycamore tree,
in the language of mice or of dandelion seeds,
or in the fabulous vowels of a whale.
How does one compose in the languages of trees?
Of bees? Of rocks rounded by water's tumbling flow?
How does one share a poem with non-human things?
It is woefully inadequate to write in human lingo
but nothing in that of the dirt or the sky or the sea,
in the idiom of slime coating the walls of a cave;
write for the apricot; write in such a way
that a sensitive toad finds it stirring.

Worldly Things

The world is a many-eyed thing,
a many-testicled, many-minded,
many many-things thing.
Our feet are the world's feet,
our noses the planet's collective
olfactory glands,
our tongues the tongues of the earth.
Lizard tongues, rabbit tongues,
tortoise tongues, aardvark tongues,
your tongue, mine:
we give this world its sense of taste
and strange articulations.
The world sees what our eyes see,
from the eyes of squirrels and
penguins and tadpoles
to your cocker spaniel and me.
It is a complex sense of sight.
It is true that spiders have many eyes,
but nothing compared to the planet's.
The same applies to its elbows,
its memories; the world's gills,
its breath and bones; its poems.
And all the other things.

I Don't Know What to Wear Today

I am the protector of imaginary friends,
the guardian of panicking rodents,
the sponsor of clouds requesting asylum.

I am the fog that lifts from time to time,
unveiling anomalies of clarity.

I am the freezing rain, the airborne allergens,
the stinging, grit-slinging whips of desert wind.

I am a quarter of an hour just passed
through which numerous sighs wistfully drifted.

I am low in fat, high in fiber, and
rich in strengthening nutrients.

I am the flatulence propelling a released balloon
so it spirals toward the ceiling, its poodle shape lost,
finally dropping to the floor, a rubber puddle of defeat.

I am a molar ground to powder,
a tongue shredded by a jagged edge,
a jawbone cracked with a hammer.

I am the misconstrued offspring of astronauts
raised by robots on the moon, tasked with learning
the alphabet song from a long-lost language.

I am the sensation of an empty stomach
of a monster roaming the sea.

I am the awfulest smell.

Despite all these mysterious wonders of who and what I am,
I still must decide which trousers to wear today.
It troubles me.

False Distinctions

These spinning atoms
only appear to be solid
much like a sequence of years
appears to be a lifetime.

Our perceptions are illusory –
a mountain is not disconnected
from the speck.

A housefly's week
and a human century
ride the same ripples
in the pond.

Blue Ink

I stain my fingers with the blue ink
of Earth as seen from space, and touch
like a priest on Ash Wednesday the faces
of passersby who walk within my reach.
Befuddled, they scurry away unaware
of the bright blue smudge of fingerprints
that marks them as terrestrial property.

The Dream

"He runs the risk of being
just a shadow on the wall"

– *narrator of a dream from which I've just awakened*

I am driving a car when two teenaged boys deliberately ride their bicycles in front of me, forcing me to brake abruptly. It is a passive-aggressive power play to show who rules the street – a street with a steep downhill slope. My brakes fail. My car races toward the boys to the terror of us all. A peripheral figure on the adjacent sidewalk comes into view. It is Justin Timberlake, strolling nonchalantly. His hands are in the pockets of his black denim trousers. Silently observing the scene, he looks on as I speed ever closer to the boys, who out of desperation are trying to pedal their bicycles backwards. And now the invisible narrator reads his line.

My Impression of Rabbits

They appear to be stupid,
which is not so much a fault
as a matter-of-fact characteristic.

After all, a tree is no critical thinker,
and I have cultivated crushes
on many a maple.

Rabbits simply scurry along
guided by a preference for silence
and edible vegetation.

They are not chatterboxes
like sparrows or squirrels.
They circuitously wriggle their faces

and quietly bop along
with minds void of thought.
What is not to admire in that?

The Man-Boy in the Well

Every boy contains his old-man-self
and within every old man dwells a boy.

Linear time overlooks
the crazy sloshing

within a multi-dimensional well
of multi-dimensional waters.

Margaret's Curtain

I am not that curtain, she insisted.
I suppose I am saying you are,
Margaret, the biologist, calmly retorted.

Everything is movement and particle and wave
inhabiting space pretending at emptiness.
There is nothing solid about what seems most solid
and nothing inert about the most still-appearing thing.

It is not that you as we perceive you
are the curtain as we perceive it
because that supposes the curtain itself
is a single thing – and you as well –
inert within boundaries.

You and I and the curtain are all a blur.
Separation among these so-called things
is an illusion, to paraphrase Einstein,
even if a stubborn one.

Don't get me started on now being then
and, like you and the curtain, tomorrow
being yesterday.

Mekong Moments

I stand on the edge of the river.
It is wide, and the water shines,
dividing two countries and patrolled
by soldiers on boats from both.
In its depths is a silent murkiness
and a current that carries corpses.

I stand on the edge of the river.
Where there is water it is stagnant, buggy.
For the most part, in this season of drought,
it is sparse and shallow. I nervously walk
in the mud toward the far, forbidden bank
but, fearful, stop just short of halfway.

I stand on the edge of the river.
A nearby fisherman calls across the water
to a man on the other side.
They laugh and wave, even though
from this distance each can barely see
the other. "We are cousins," he explains.

I stand on the edge of the river.
It carries frightened children's chatter
in a language of the hills. Their mother
coos to her baby to calm her own fears.
The father is silent and strains as he
pulls the family's raft while he swims.

I stand on the edge of the river.
The border is open now, the taboos history.
How strange to witness the ease of traffic
crossing in both directions. Past horrors
seem surreal and tragically absurd.
The water does its job and flows.

The World Has Other Eyes with Which to See

The world has other eyes with which to see,
other tongues with which to speak,
and other working brains with which to speculate.

In vain I seek solace in this notion as your own eyes grow dim,
your tongue increasingly awkward,
your mind steadily less adept.

Still, I cannot help but think that the world will note
with shudders of loss an abrupt downward shift
in its strange imagination when you're gone,

its friendship with creative dissidents,
its sense of responsibility toward their poverty;
and also, sentimentally, its love for cats and coffee.

We must gird ourselves
to strive, the Earth and I,
to compensate.

Zoom Lens

Zoom in and see
your friend's
dying.
Zoom out
and hypothesize
that the whole
mesmerizing
juxtaposition
of lifespans
with their
gasp-filled endings
streaming through
this seemingly
infinite sequence
of biographies,
is one complex
moment
immune to gains
or losses,
one profoundly
singular
unfolding.
Zoom in
to grieve.
Zoom out.

Spending This Day Like Monopoly Money

Mostly in solitude
slowly drinking copious
quantities of hot tea
cup by small cup,
dozing between pots,
bored, lonely, restless,
slightly depressed –
I am so much more
intensely fortunate
than so many other
inhabitants of this time
in the world spent
mostly in solitude,
most without their own
small cups filled
throughout the day
with servings of tea as
the silent sun slides by.

(Christmas Day, 2019)

I Am Not in Alberta Today

But I feel the solid mountain slab
hard beneath my sneakers
like when I stepped upon that massive rock
at age fourteen in Banff. I am as far today
from being fourteen as I am from the heft
of glacier-carved mountains upon which I once stood.
I am actually not wearing sneakers today, much less
hiking on a giant mountain. Gently I press the accelerator
of my Toyota to exit the parking lot
of a neighborhood restaurant. Beneath me rises
the surface of the mountain as I ease my foot on the gas.
Is this a wormhole, favorite plot device of science fiction,
folding the time-space continuum, that positions me
in two locations and moments at once?
Or maybe some ice-slick spot of disassociation?
Is that distinction relevant as I navigate
another fleeting blink of simultaneous everything?

January 1

As we mark another trip around the sun
(an ordinary star among at least billions),

we wheel through what seems like a huge swath of space but which
in truth is a puny microcosm of impossible-to-fathom enormity.

Our shadows shrink until they disappear;
and then they start to lengthen once again.

Whether we watch them and notice or not
the sun, the moon, the light, the shadows

the journey, the dance, the vast expanse –
they carry on and on, and here we are

improbably riding along, a part of the phenomenon
through measured years of fleeting moments.

He Sleeps Beneath a Box

with the wind and the rain
and the heat and the snow
and the glare and the cover
of clouds in the night
and reflections of rays
of the sun from the moon
and the noise and the light
and the silence of shadows
and stillness and whirl
of the mind of a man
looking up looking in
looking out looking
drowsily nowhere.

Early December

Is there truly, in the end, such a thing as a brown sweater? Worn much less by a figure in a round hat? This figure whistles until realizing it is the melody from an old song that he or she despises. The sick wind blows with a biting cold that seems unjust.

Given a Chance to Fly

I would not resist the chance
to bend the laws of gravity

long enough to rise into the sky and sail
to my childhood home, hovering

above the yard behind the red brick house,
looking down at my eight-year-old self

as he stands with open upturned hands
beneath a massive maple tree

and waits to catch the spinning whirlybirds
that fall from the tree with its seeds,

being his true glad self, fully enchanted
and joyously blind to airborne me.

There Will Be Moonlight Casting Shadows on the Empty Streets

There will be heavy sighs and weeping, ugly flashes of fear-fed greed, and impulsive acts of hoarding, while they last, of random things. There will be restlessness, monotony, and lonely swallowed thoughts. There will be moments of detachment and of panic, longing, and fatigue. There will be listless devotion to mundane routines. There will be anonymous humility, poignant generosity, troubled sleep, and frivolous distractions. At any given moment there will be the unexpected sound of laughter, and briefly, somewhere in the world, an outburst of spontaneous dancing.

Even the Doves are Restless

The sight of doves through the kitchen window is a rare treat, but these birds are bored. Bored, even, with their own songs; reluctant to release the most tentative of warbles lest they be mistaken for expressions of joy. They simply squat on the eaves, low over their feet, shifting from one to another as if they have gum on the bottoms of their shoes. The pea-brained sparrows scattered in the trees and clutching power lines chatter away, oblivious to the gloomy mood. In contrast, these plump, pale doves seem to be here against their will. They silently swallow their would-be coos, eyes darting this way, that, that way, this. Anticipating more of the same, they squirm in their feathers, trapped, morose, disgruntled, too heart-heavy to fly away.

It is Strange to See Time Bend and Then Break

Long, long ago we were each other's deep entanglement;
first love can be a beautiful lunacy,
intense and formative to young incapable selves.

Later we'd come to experience, after the heartbreak,
awkward kinds of growth, the intensity diminishing
despite our expectations.

Melodrama finally evaporates and there is a maturing;
years follow years and love mellows into quietly smiling memory
over time, time that becomes increasingly at one with distance.

Decades pass. Today, I learn that she has died;
I am told she thought of reaching out to me as she was dying;
she never did, so someone else is left to make the call now,
someone else's voice that says hello.

It is strange for the heart to learn of an old flame's death,
and strange to see on this sleepless night's ceiling
sweetly familiar shadows gracefully dancing,
cast by the last flickering light of that old flame –

one final whisper of fire.

Now that You are What We Call Dead

My interest
in talking with you again
is clarified now that
it is impossible.

It is difficult
to stop wishing
and to shake
the obvious insight
that we could have
been more important
to each other
than our history,
our resting
on the knowledge
of the distant past.

Now the less remote past
is here to haunt us –
or, I guess, just me –
for failing to go
beyond the assumption
that we-can-reconnect-at-
any-time, as if sensing it
while passively ignoring it
is somehow enough.

We know, and we have
always known, that
it is not enough.
What a foolish betrayal
of the heart's simple truth.

Importing the Plague

Spiders piloting a ship
through dense fog into a harbor
unwittingly carry on their sticky feet
the traces of a pestilence.

Once in port the spiders inaudibly shriek
as grotesque, unshaven humans
of diminutive wit clamber aboard.
To these oafs it is a ghost ship.
They stomp about,
ignoring the offended arachnids
whose webs stick onto their
tongue-mopped faces
as they tear through the structures
of fine silk thread engineered
throughout the ship.

Like ogres they pillage the vessel for rum
and go home drunk in the afternoon
with its stink on their breath.
The dullards carry across their thresholds
their newly acquired brides,
invisible sweethearts of Plague.
This hamlet will not enjoy
a happy ending.

(The fates of the spiders themselves
will be varied and legendary,
tales better wondered at than told.)

The Musical Blur of Time

If we dismantle the construct of time and blur Before, After, and Now, birth, living, and death become a simultaneous unfolding. This leaves open the question of what, then, is grief and joy, disaster and triumph? Do they have their proper places? Or are they, too, dismantled?

Possibly. Or possibly they belong to a symphonic context – the remarkable rising crescendo of trumpets, flutes, oboes, French horns, violins, and xylophones, crashes of cymbals and barely audible triangle dings, along with the silent movement of the cellist's fingers as they unconsciously rise to her face to tuck some loosened hair behind her ear just before she presses her bow into and across the calibrated strings, releasing her instrument's somber expression of truth.

One grand moment of everything.

Cutting the Grass Among Grackles

As I mow the lawn a small harem of grackles descends. One large male with a blue-black sheen vociferously announces himself. Three smaller, dull-colored females tag along. As a group they stalk me while I circumnavigate the yard with my noisy machine. The birds pace to my side a few feet away, the females unobtrusively, the male with showy stomps. At times they break into agitated hops. They dig in the dirt where my lawn-mower's spinning blade has just cut the green grass short. They also wade through the unmowed portions exhibiting impatience. The harem-master periodically scolds me with a squawk. I greet them all with "Hello, budgies," which goes unacknowledged. I can't help but feel a little snubbed. By the time I finish mowing and silence the engine, the birds ignore me. Still pacing. Still hopping. Probing for grubs with their thin black beaks. I reflect that my small realm is more complex than I usually notice, a microcosm of the biosphere. In my way I also dig for insects and warn away with noise would-be intruders of my nearby nest. Pushing the quiet mower, I nod at the birds in an unrequited gesture of respect and depart with a hop.

Hypothesis: Faith

In light of infinite time and space
with a proposed nature
of absolute overlap

the moral laws that define this moment
but are not universal
reveal themselves to be a hoax.

But sometimes a hoax provides comfort
in that without guidance
a vaguely conscious mind loses trust.

Without trust in one's nature,
with the limitations of perspective
that are inevitable for biological creatures

who identify themselves
as discrete units of character
relying on dramatic scenarios

to pilot themselves through
the peculiarities
of the Moment,

it can sometimes be
a scary
ride.

Six Pounds of Pressure

In a gesture of liberation, he pulls at his hospital bracelet.
The plastic stretches until it breaks. Discharged from the psychiatric unit,
he sits with me now in this small, drab office, invisibly reeling
behind a mask of composure.

I unfurl before him the bureaucratic banner of endless questions,
signatures, and explanations. "This is a process," I half-apologize.

I thank him for his patience and carefully lead him through the assessment.
He exhibits a combination of tension and relief, as if sucking in air
after minutes of holding his breath.

His voice sharpens its cutting edge as he mentions his several deployments.
"I will never talk," he predicts, "about the last one."

He is nervous about the halfway house where he's agreed to stay.
Group living. Roommates. He doesn't trust his anger.
"If someone comes at me," he says not with fear. "I'll lose it."
I see him playing it out in his head, reacting to an imagined assailant.
Throwing him down, breaking his arm.

"I wouldn't even think. It's automatic. I was trained..."
I assure him, "Nobody there is looking for a fight."

He informs me that it only takes six pounds of pressure to break a wrist.
"Just like that!" he adds, pushing down on his own hand.
He seems amazed by how expert he has become in the art of doing damage.

His voice thickens and tears begin when he talks about relationships –
three imploded marriages before the age of forty.

"I am so damn broken," he confesses. Then he shakes his head
and forces a laugh. "They say I need at least a year of therapy.
Maybe even a year and a half!"

I revisit what he told me about breaking a wrist.
"It just takes a second, right? Then days of pain and weeks of healing.
You said it yourself: you feel like you're broken. More than a broken wrist.
Your injuries are like those of the survivor of a parachute accident."

I read his face: memories are rushing through his head.
It is no small feat for a brain to consider everything hard and beautiful
it has gone through, simultaneously.

I usher him through the rest of my questions, the forms, the signatures.
By the time we're done, he has settled into a tentative readiness.

The trust of a fragile man is like receiving a handmade gift.

I smile. "We're done for today," I proclaim. "Let's get you settled in."
He nods and stands. I take him to the house of broken bones.

Court Reporter

I listen intently
to each low of the cow
as she testifies
from the pasture
just beyond the fence.

Strawberries and Snowballs

What alien gardener poked into your brain the strange and terrible seeds that have sprouted, instead of strawberries, flourishing tumors? They enlarge themselves like snowballs rolling down a hill.

Strawberries like the ones we devoured by the basket in Maymyo. Snowballs like those you would toss in the air as a boy.

[Captive in the ICU with hands bound in mittens, he longs to be home with his cats and his coffee, his manuscripts and his malignancy.]

We should go to Burma again, my friend. To Laos. To Phitsanulok at midnight. To upstate New York. To Ubon. To 1985.

Memories unattached to your disease.

Charm Me Tonight, My Love

Compare me to a serpent's swaying hips;
regale me with tales of snowflakes
that ascend instead of falling.

Recite to me an ode to the achievements
of a bat, to clouds beneath the ocean,
and to turnips on the moon.

Whisper-sing a hymn in heartfelt praise
of hairless cats and laugh
among the joyful stones of silence.

Summer Sounds

Bitching little birds
tussle over seeds
scattered on the ground.

Eyes drowsily blinking,
the panting dog suddenly snaps
at a pesky fly.

We barely hear
the mechanical clicks and hums
of the air coming on.

Halving a hefty melon,
the long knife hits the cutting board
like a guillotine.

Invisible cicadas
collectively obliterate
the afternoon's silence.

A quintessentially metallic
scraping and pop –
aluminum cans open with a hiss.

Two chatting neighbors
share beer on the porch
in friendly laughter.

After the sun goes down,
randy cats perform their raunchy opera –
screams and melodrama.

Like a battering ram
thunder splinters the night –
an unexpected summer storm.

Rebellion of the Fatalistic Monk

The fatalistic monk eats an ice cream;
relaxing from detached observation,
he savors its cool smooth sweetness
and the waffle cone's crunch.

The fatalistic monk
staring at the candle flame
leans towards it surreptitiously
when he's about to sneeze.

During meditation
the fatalistic monk
pretends he is flying
in a spaceship.

The fatalistic monk
has long abandoned
his pursuit of enlightenment,
wondering if anyone has noticed.

You May Have Heard This Before

Forgive me for repeating myself:
you are a beautiful woman.
It is difficult
not to continue singing that song.

Repose in the Time of the Apocalypse

Sit on a wall
swinging your legs
as you look at the sea
or look at the grass
and imagine the sea.
Catch yourself
humming a song
from your childhood
you didn't know
you remember.

Try not to believe
that we can't choose
to be heroes of change.
Rest, but rest from
hopelessness.
Find a way to sing
and make a fist.
Ready yourself
for a slug-out
with complacency.

Meanwhile
sit on the wall
swinging your legs
as you look
at what's there
and at what
would be better
and isn't there yet.

When you are ready
hop down from
the wall.

When Life Loves Life to Death

Deeply moved by passion,
Life copulates with Life,
implanting Life's fertile seed
in Life's uterine paradise.
"Ohhh, Life!" moans Life.

Life's swollen belly
shelters and incubates
Life's sprouting seed
until gestation is complete.
Finally Life gives birth
to a baby, Death, the child
of Life and Life.

"Life!" calls Life to Life
with exhaustion and joy.
"Look at our perfect child!
Our Death looks just like you!"

Discovery

On your morning walk, pause
when you see a small rock.
Squat down and study it.
Pick it up and stare at its mineral veins,
its meandering edges, its asymmetry.

With a surge of growing excitement
glance around, and if nobody's looking
pocket it. Resume walking,
face stretched involuntarily
into an irrepressible grin.

You may find that your strides are longer,
your pace more swift, your trajectory
redirected toward your house.
Once there you rush inside,
find a private room, and close the door.

Remove that stone from your pocket.
Gaze at it in the palm of your hand.
Hold it to the light like it's a diamond
you unearthed in your garden.

Marvel astonished at your fabulous luck:
an ordinary rock found floating
in outer space!

Aphorisms

1

I love what fog
allows me to see.

2

Solstice reminds us
of all the moving parts.

3

When despair awakens tenderness,
sad gladness weeps.

4

During the Cold War too many
children drew crayon trees
that looked like mushroom clouds.

5

Humans're okay when it comes
especially to particular ones.

6

Pain and anger
make the same soup.

7

The moon is a world
longing for a moon.

8

It is better to stare at the clouds
while on a hilltop than at one's feet.

9

A temple's sonorous gong
is the antidote
to a jangling brain.

10

Slippery and hazardous is time underfoot,
waving our arms to keep balance our little ballet.

11

Too few boys are haunted
by their wanton destruction of anthills.

12

Earth will be blind
once the last of its beasts
having eyes finally dies.

13

Of all the hallucinations,
false whiffs of odor provide
for the gentlest form
of psychosis.

14

We can all
become elderly
if we try
long enough.

15

Sometimes even when we smell it
it is hard to acknowledge the rot.

16

Even bisected earthworms
are called to dance.

17

The raging wind is
today's
Nostradamus.

18

The first biological instant and the last – the initial kick-start of a heart and its final thud – and all that unfolds in between – from far enough back, is all one Mighty Blink.

19

Consider the egg:
encapsulated flight.

20

Nibbling on a moment,
one tastes the whole
of history.

21

We miss the sweet smell of magnolias
when swimming in the deep.

22

If you want to hear yourself echo,
holler into a canyon:
O torn kites lost in the wind!

23

No child
should be chastised
for bad origami.

24

A crumpled ball of paper
is a contour map
of time and space.

25

A well-constructed yurt
can nicely accommodate
a lifetime's collection of wishes.

26

The unique joy
of ululating women
leaps across meadows
like a startled doe.

27

The truest aphorism
is a question.

Rhetorical Questions

What has become of the girl I saw
thirty years ago sitting on the stairs
with her head in her hands, motionless
except for her long cigarette's
rising thread of smoke?

Why is the phrase
"teasing a parrot"
so utterly charming?

Is it feasible that the playmate
whose arm I once petted like a cat,
transfixed, when we both were four
has spent her life craving
my fascinated affection?

Do we inhabit this planet
or are we, like methane gas,
one of its excretions?

What tattoo
best represents
every forgotten thing?

What chords accompany
a dream's evaporation?

What color dog embodies
the transmutability
of clouds?

Is there such a thing
as a lifetime squandered
for a fish, a mouse, a tree?
For a fungus, say, or a wren;
an orangutan, a poet, a bean?

What vivid scenes might emerge
in a puddle after the rain?

Observing a bird break its neck
on a window
takes one's breath away;
what of roasted duck?

Having fallen into a well are you
moved to dive, swimming to the
bottom in order to kiss the mud?

Which of the fish in the sea
is impossible?

If Everywhere is limitlesss
and Somewhere its subset,
can there be a Nowhere-at-all?

When does the sight of the moon
cease to be a surprise?

Is the mind a sieve through which
reality is filtered as it pours,
or a mysterious, sloshing bucket
holding all of time?

Is time a liquid
mistaken for ice,
or a gas?

What curious monkey
cannot learn how
to open the package
containing itself?

In the silent hour of Always,
is existence but a sneeze?

With all of the wheres and the whens
what has become of the whos?

What if all of time
is somehow
simultaneous?

Questions About Snakes

What do snakes
assume about animals
with visible ears?

As they slither in the dust,
do they ever have
fits of sneezing?

Do snakes' eyes cross
when admiring
their tongues?

Do snakes
have dreams
of flying?

Do they carry
wallets
made of mice?

How desperate
would a snake be
to drink its own poison?

What does it mean
to a snake
to have no legs?

Do snakes
have a theory
of the afterlife?

Do snakes reminisce
about the lost tree
of knowledge?

What – ?

What is this machine?
This mechanical muscle?
This brilliant shock of green?

What is this queasiness?
This tingling of the lip?
This half-remembered song?

What is this hairy heart?
This heavy fruit?
This bony thing?

What is this airy song?
This monolingualism?
This semi-melted stone?

What moving objects
are casting this circus show
of shadows?

What is this rumbling sound?
This disembodiment?
This frantic ambition to fly?

What are these
contradictions?
What is this ice-cold key?
What is this spinning disk

on which nimble fingers
are shaping a generous dollop
of mud into a pitcher for milk

squeezed without consent
from the teats of a goat?
And what is this mighty tree

that gently moans?
What, I ask, is this
simultaneous everything?

Acknowledgments & Other Notes

Near the end of his life, poet and novelist Richard Wright composed hundreds of haiku, which were published posthumously in **Haiku: The Last Poems of an American Icon** (Arcade Publishing). The poem "Court Reporter" draws from one of those haiku: *Why do I listen / to each low of the cow / this still autumn night?* The wall-sitting image in "Repose in the Time of the Apocalypse" is borrowed from Tony Hoagland's poem "Into the Mystery." The sequence "Rhetorical Questions" owes a debt to Pablo Neruda's **Libro de las Preguntas** (The Book of Questions).

Thanks are extended to all who offered suggestions in various stages of drafting this collection. Similarly, heart-felt gratitude extends to anyone who reads these poems and in doing so makes the creative act complete.

Author's proceeds from the sales of this book will go to New Creation Lifework, a non-profit organization providing sober living opportunities for individuals seeking to make positive change.

About the Poet

Kevin Acers is a cat person. He has been an educator, a human rights advocate, a Peace Corps Volunteer, a social worker, and all the while a poet. This is his sixth book, published on the occasion of his sixtieth birthday. His writings have appeared in numerous literary journals and other publications. Two of his previous books have been selected as finalists for the Oklahoma Book Award. He lives in Oklahoma City with his wife, their cat, and a tubercular potted plant named Fronds Kafka.

Made in the USA
Middletown, DE
13 October 2020

21871218R00071